Hangin' With
Aaron Carter

By Michael-Anne Johns

Scholastic Inc.

New York   Toronto   London   Auckland   Sydney

Mexico City   New Delhi   Hong Kong   Buenos Aires

Back cover: Joseph Galea; Page 6: Joseph Galea; Page 7: (left) Arnold Turner; (right) Arnold Turner; Page 8: (top) Arnold Turner; (middle) Arnold Turner; Page 11: Joseph Galea; Page 12: (left) Joseph Galea; (right) Joseph Galea; Page 14: Joseph Galea; Page 18: (left) Joseph Galea; (right) Joseph Galea; Page 19: Ron Wolfson/London Features International; Page 20: (bottom) Arnold Turner; Page 21: (top) Ron Wolfson/London Features International; (bottom) Ron Wolfson/London Features International; Page 22: (left) Joseph Galea; (right) Joseph Galea; Page 23: Joseph Galea; Pages 24-25: Joseph Galea; Page 27: Arnold Turner; Page 33: Arnold Turner; Page 34: (top) Arnold Turner; (bottom) Arnold Turner; Page 35: Arnold Turner; Page 36: (top) Arnold Turner; (bottom) Arnold Turner; Page 37: Arnold Turner; Page 40: (top left) Arnold Turner; (bottom right) Arnold Turner; Page 41: Arnold Turner; Page 42: (left) Steve Granitz/Retna; (right) Steve Granitz/Retna; Page 43: (top left) Steve Granitz/Retna; (bottom left) Steve Granitz/Retna; (right) Steve Granitz/Retna; Page 44: (right) Arnold Turner; Page 45: (top left) Arnold Turner; (bottom left) Steve Granitz/Retna; Page 47: Jeffrey Mayer/Star File Photo.

ISBN 0-439-32693-1

Designed by Carisa Swenson
Photo Editor: Sharon Lennon

12 11 10 9 8 7 6 5 4   1 2 3 4 5 6/0
Printed in U.S.A.
First Scholastic printing, September 2001

Contents

Come to the party! Which party?
Aaron Carter's life!

The platinum-crowned Prince of Pop sends you an invitation to join the good times, which actually began four years ago when a ten-year-old Aaron first opened for his big brother. And who is his big brother? Nick Carter of the Backstreet Boys, of course. That was way back in 1997, when Aaron made his debut before a German audience. After that, a European record company spotted his talent and scooped him up. He signed on the dotted line and in the following two years broke all sorts of music chart records, selling millions of albums and singles. In Europe, he was dubbed "the Little Prince of Pop."

The festivities continued when Aaron released his second CD, *Aaron's Party (Come Get It)*, in the United States on September 26, 2000. Indeed, months later Aaron received a crazy-cool Christmas present when *Aaron's Party* went platinum, music-industry speak for selling one million copies!

Well, these days the pint-sized hottie's album has gone multi-platinum, and he's still in the party mode. On the following pages, you'll be able to share the good times with Aaron as we follow him around for some fun. You'll be able to check out what it's like to attend an Aaron Carter concert, hang with his friends and family, and even share a peek at some candid photos. So join the fun, fun, fun . . . come get it!

Free Passes to Aaron in Concert!

When Aaron gets on stage, he's at his happiest. The minute he hears the applause from the audience, Aaron is in his element and there's no keeping him down. So bounce with the boy as he sings his heart out!

"Usually I spent about seven hours a day in the studio," Aaron recalls of the time he recorded *Aaron's Party (Come Get It)*. "It was fun." But when it was finished, Aaron was ready to hit the stage and hit the road for a concert tour!

"Sometimes I get nervous before a show," Aaron admits. "It depends on how big the crowd is. Actually, the smaller the crowd the scarier it is. It's just because you can see the people more and all of them looking at you."

7

Aaron loves to sing "I Want Candy" — except when the fans throw hard candy on stage and hit him. It definitely keeps the Air Boy on his toes!

Aaron and his crew give a big shout-out to the audience.

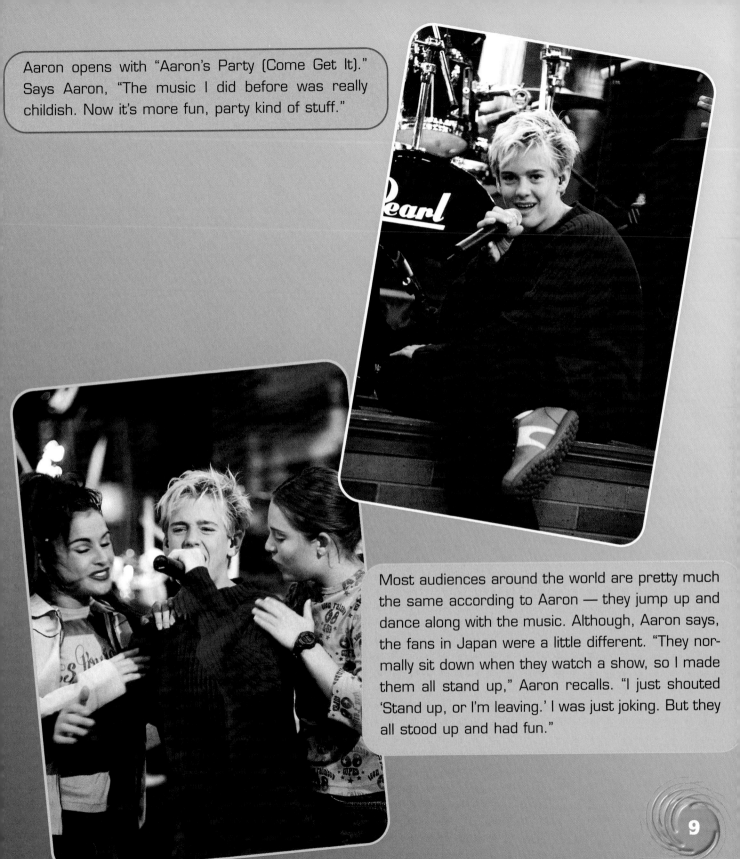

Aaron opens with "Aaron's Party (Come Get It)." Says Aaron, "The music I did before was really childish. Now it's more fun, party kind of stuff."

Most audiences around the world are pretty much the same according to Aaron — they jump up and dance along with the music. Although, Aaron says, the fans in Japan were a little different. "They normally sit down when they watch a show, so I made them all stand up," Aaron recalls. "I just shouted 'Stand up, or I'm leaving.' I was just joking. But they all stood up and had fun."

Bye, bye!

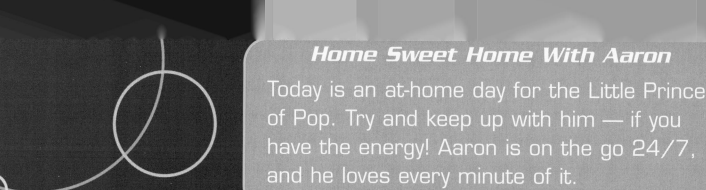

Home Sweet Home With Aaron

Today is an at-home day for the Little Prince of Pop. Try and keep up with him — if you have the energy! Aaron is on the go 24/7, and he loves every minute of it.

Aaron's day starts with a phone check of his appointments. They could include interviews, photo shoots, promotional appearances, and the like. Aaron particularly likes it when he's heading off for a concert tour. "I love traveling and I get to do a lot of it when I'm on tour," he says.

Music is second nature to Aaron. He's been singing since he was just a tyke, and he started playing instruments when he began elementary school. Here, Aaron shows off the keyboard brother Nick gave to him as a birthday present. His next instrument? "I want to learn how to play the saxophone," Aaron says. "I've always had one, but I'm just trying to learn it now."

Mmmm! Aaron will be the first to tell you that his favorite eats is a McDonald's Special — a Big Mac, fries, and Coca-Cola . . . supersized! But eating in bed?!! You know his mom isn't going to be happy about that — watch out for the crumbs, Aaron!

Believe it or not, this boy in the shower claims he used to be bashful. "A long time ago, when I was in school, I used to be very shy," Aaron confesses. "When the teacher called on me, I'd talk in a quiet voice, way below normal. My teacher, Mrs. Matthews, helped me. She'd keep me after school and talk to me. She told me not to be so scared." Guess it worked!

One of Aaron's favorite songs on his CD *Aaron's Party (Come Get It)* is the love ballad, "Tell Me What You Want." Always ready to share an acoustic version on his guitar, Aaron explains: "It's pretty much . . . about giving people another chance. It's about people who break up and get back together, but still don't have a great relationship. The words are complicated, and I'm not sure I even understand everything the song is saying! But I know I've gone through it . . . many times."

Aaron visits cities all over the country . . . the world, actually . . . and he always checks out what's happening and hot in town. But even in Fun City—The Big Apple—Aarons' heart is back home in California!

Scrapbook Secrets — Bouncin' Through the Years With Aaron

When Aaron is playing "the host with the most" for guests at his home, he might pull out some photos to show you . . . or if they are baby pictures, his mom, Jane, might let you sneak a peek!

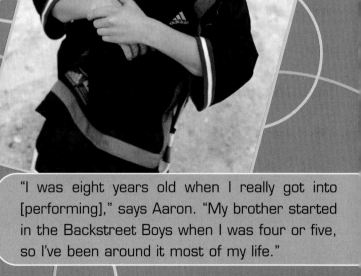

"I was eight years old when I really got into [performing]," says Aaron. "My brother started in the Backstreet Boys when I was four or five, so I've been around it most of my life."

Aaron's always liked to party, although when he was a little kid, "party" meant being a daredevil at the playground!

As a little guy growing up in Tampa, Florida, Aaron developed a love of water sports. He swims like a fish, loves snorkeling and diving, and now is trying to catch a wave surfing.

Awww! Here's Aaron at age ten.

18

Welcome to the Carters' Florida home! From left to right: Dad Robert, Aaron, sisters Leslie, Angel, and Bobbie Jean. Aaron would love to start a group with his siblings. He'd call them the "Carter Five"!

Here's Aaron with his mom and a family friend. Jane Carter is Aaron's co-manager.

welve. Growing up is fun to when you get to hang out with ck Lachey, Jessica Simpson, and e. Just ask Aaron!

Aaron plays with his best pal, dog Oscar.

A real dog lover, Aaron cuddles two of his family's pups!

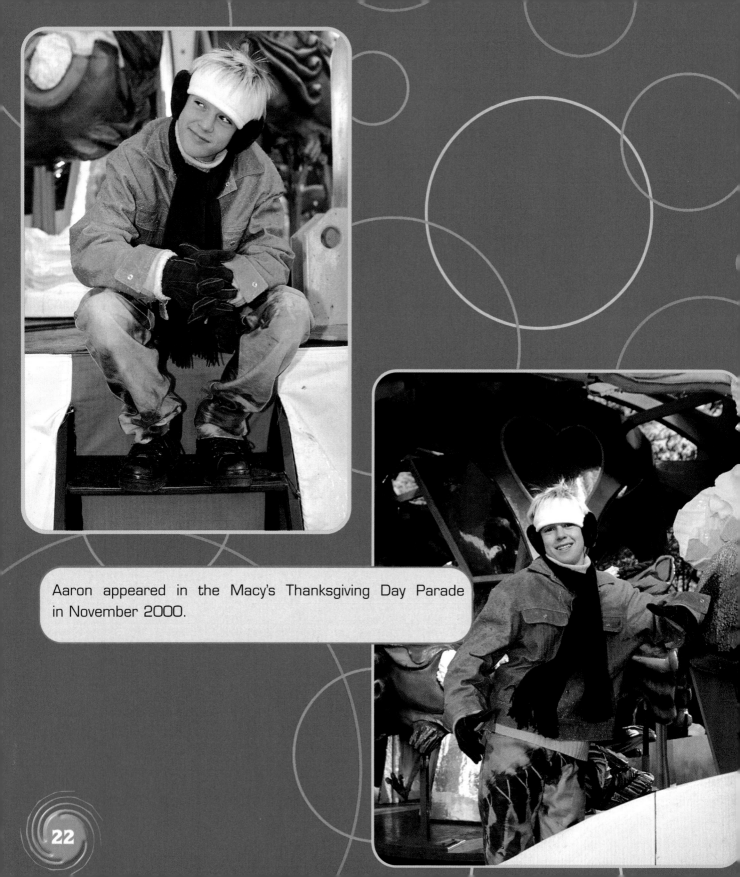

Aaron appeared in the Macy's Thanksgiving Day Parade in November 2000.

Here's Aaron at age thirteen. He says, "Without Nick I don't think I could have made it [to] where I am right now."

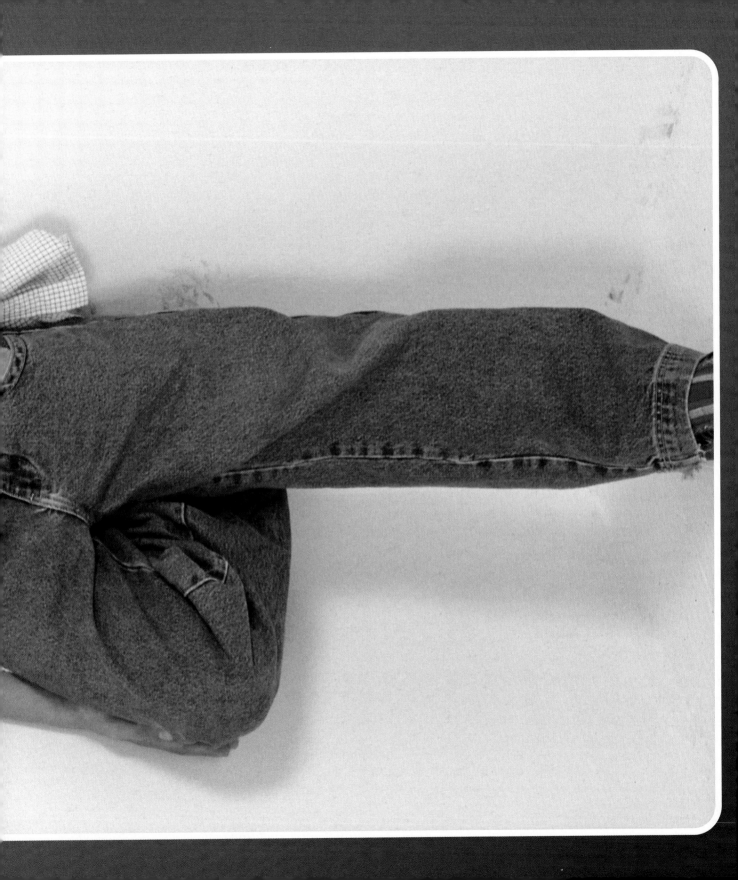

Aaron's Ultimate Personal Printout

Aaron—In His Own Handwriting

MIDDLE NAME: _Charles_

NICKNAME: (Who gave it to you & why _Little Prince of Pop (and England record Co.)_

BIRTHDATE: _12 · 7 · 87_

BIRTHPLACE: _Tampa FL._

CURRENT RESIDENCE: _Marina Del Ray_

RIGHTY OR LEFTY? _Righty_

HEIGHT: _5' 2"_

WEIGHT: _90_

HAIR & EYE COLOR: _Blond, Brown_

PARENTS: _Robert + Jane_

SIBLINGS & AGES: _Nick (20), Bobbie Jean (18), Leslie (14) Angel (12) Twin_

CHILDHOOD PETS: _Oscar, Merlin, Simba_

PRESENT PETS: _Simba, Oscar_

BEST FRIEND: _Paul Webster_

DESCRIBE YOURSELF AS A CHILD: _Played alot very mischivious played lots of sports_

Aaron penned this printout in the summer of 2000

Fabulous Faves

Sports: Motocross, basketball, fishing, racing boats, surfing

Sports Team: Oakland A's (baseball); Tampa Bay Buccaneers (football)

Possession: His collection of motorcycles and dirt bikes

Motorcycle: Kawasaki KX80

Pet: His weimaraner Oscar — "He's like a son to me!"

TV Shows: *Friends*, *South Park*, *Frasier*

Classic Movie: *Stand By Me*

Actor/Actress: Sly Stallone, Sandra Bullock

Bands: Metallica, 'N Sync, Backstreet Boys

Singer: Jessica Simpson

Rapper: Will Smith — "Because he sings about positive stuff."

Car: Viper

Foods: Sushi, pizza (Aaron's least fave food is broccoli)

Fast Food: McDonald's

Drinks: Blue Gatorade, Sprite, iced tea

Candy: Twix

Donuts: Krispy Kreme

Sandwich: Bacon, lettuce, and tomato

Historical Era: 1960s

Chewing Gum: Bubblelicious

Ice Cream: Chocolate

Cereal: Count Chocula

Toothpaste: Rembrandt

Fashion Designer: Tommy Hilfiger

Shoes: Air Jordans — he has more than twenty pairs

Colors: Green and blue

School Subject: Science

Book: Harry Potter series

Fictional Character: Robin Hood

After School Snack: Fruit Rollups

Collections: Beanie Babies, Pokémon Cards, Ninja Turtles, baseball cards, antique pennies he got from his father

Board Game: Monopoly

Video Games: PlayStation's James Bond, Mario, Megaman

Number: 7

Jewelry: A ring given to him by a friend — "I really don't take it off. It gives me good luck."

Halloween Costume: The pumpkin costume his mom made for him "because I could stick my arms in and hide inside of it."

Animals: Tigers and wolves

Holidays: His birthday and Christmas

Country Visited: Argentina

Phrase: "Anyway"

Fantastic Firsts

Theme Park Visited: Disney World

Movie: *Land Before Time*

Concert: Janet Jackson

CD Bought: Ninja Turtles

Trip Out of the Country: Malaysia

Crush: "I had a crush on this girl called Briana when I was about six and I got in trouble for kissing her."

Girlfriend: A girl named Jackie — they met on the set of Aaron's video "Shake It." They aren't together anymore.

Band: Dead End — Aaron was in elementary school in Tampa when they got together.

Top 10

1) Most Embarrassing Moment: "Ummm . . . when I was in a grocery store in the vegetable aisle, I picked up a fruit and just started eating it, and my grandma came over and started yelling at me in front of all my friends."

2) Most Embarrassing Video: "The video my mom has of me and my twin sister, Angel, jumping on the couch singing 'Twist and Shout.'"

3) Prediction: *People* magazine listing him in their "What's Next 2001" feature.

4) Weirdest Thing He's Ever Eaten: "Octopus. And I like sardines and anchovies. I eat them on crackers, and sometimes I even eat the sardines with vanilla ice cream!"

5) Silliest Moment: When he got his toe stuck up the water tap in the tub. "I had to pull and pull until it popped out. It hurt but I didn't cry. I've got a scar on my foot."

6) Best Baseball Card: "My signed Mickey Mantle card."

7) If I Could Be An Animal . . . : "I'd be a cat so I could climb every-where."

8) Place To Read: "I have a really cozy leather chair in my room. First it was my mom's, but then I took it and now it's in my room."

9) Childhood Memory: "Fishing with my family in Florida."

10) Future Fantasy: To get some tattoos — "A dragon on my back, an 'I love Mom' on my left arm, and a mean-looking smiley face on my forearm."

Where Has Aaron Acted?

1) *HiFi Room* (Fox Family)

2) *Sabrina the Teenage Witch* (WB)

3) *Rocket Power* (Nickelodeon)

4) *Lizzie McGuire* (Disney Channel)

5) *Blackrock* — a 1997 movie (Aaron played a surfer)

Aaron was the Favorite Rising Star at this year's Nickelodeon Kid's Choice Awards!

Video Games
"That's How I Beat Shaq"

During early June 2000 Aaron Carter was busy, busy, busy. He was putting the finishing touches on his first album for Jive Records, Aaron's Party (Come Get It), and filming five videos for his home video release, Aaron's Party (Come Get It) — the Videos. The series included "Aaron's Party (Come Get It)," "Iko Iko," "The Clapping Song," "I Want Candy," and "Bounce." Now, you get front row seats for the filming of Aaron's video "That's How I Beat Shaq," the second single from Aaron's CD.

A major basketball fan, Aaron had a crazy time hangin' out with — and hangin' on — NBA super-star Shaquille O'Neal of the Los Angeles Lakers. According to Aaron, it was a slam dunk!

33

The video takes you through a day with b-ball boy Aaron — he lives for basketball! He even dreams about basketball and wakes up ready to make a hook shot!

Aaron zips over to play hoops on his Razor scooter — can't get there fast enough!

Cheered on by his own cheerleaders, Aaron leads them in a rap!

Anyone for a little one-on-one? Aaron's ready to challenge all comers.

"It was really fun," Aaron says of working with Shaq on the video. "I had a good time with him. He's a really nice guy — he's really down to earth, just a really nice guy."

Fantastic Aaron

The minute Aaron shows his face, fans seem to appear out of nowhere . . . and Aaron loves every minute of it! He really digs making personal appearances and meeting fans from everywhere. Join Aaron for a busy day of meeting and greeting!

The day starts out with an appearance on ABC-TV's *Good Morning America*. Aaron chats with host Charlie Gibson.

After *Good Morning America* Aaron goes to an autograph signing session for his CD, *Aaron's Party (Come Get It)*.

And before he heads to the next appearance, Aaron personalizes some posters for his fans.

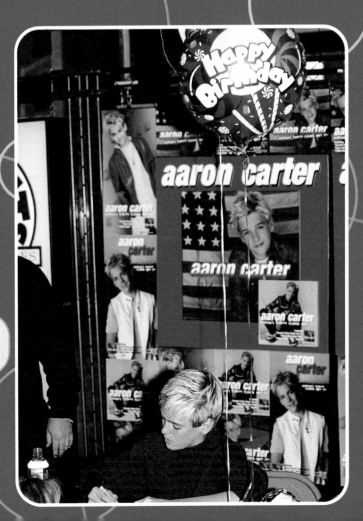

Here's Aaron at a book signing for his mom's book, *Little Prince of Pop*. Aaron admits he was kind of embarrassed about the book at first. "But I'm cool about it now," he says.

Aaron's ready and willing to sign copies of his mom's book until they are all sold out!

Aaron leaps for joy after the book signing for *Little Prince of Pop* at Borders Bookstore. He just made so many fans so happy!

Aaron & Nick — Pop in a Photo Booth

Aaron is only thirteen years old and already a superstar . . . and on top of that, he gets to hang out with his mega-star older bro, Nick. Those Carter boys have a lot of talent, and a lot of brotherly love. So you could share the fun, we framed a moment in time with Aaron and Nick. Check it out!

"When I was little, I used to be jealous of Nick, because I wasn't out there on the road having fun," Aaron confesses. "But now I am, and it's really cool!"

Asked if he would like to work with any other singer, Aaron was quick to answer, "Britney Spears and my brother. I don't have any plans right now, but I hope to do that someday."

Aaron and Nick are no strangers to cameras. When Nick first joined BSB, he loved to make mini-videos and Aaron usually starred in them. Though not Oscar material, Aaron says they were unforgettable — unfortunately. "Nick embarrassed me in one of his movies," Aaron recalls. "It was [like] a Rambo movie and I was like a little Rambo guy. Guess what Nick did? He took it out on the road and showed it to everybody!"

Aaron may want to have his own identity, but Nick will never let him forget who's the big brother. "He's very energetic and crazy," Nick laughs as he clowns around with Aaron. "That's my little brother!"

Aaron is proud to say that he's learned a lot from Nick, but he's determined not to use his brother's fame to make his mark. "I am Nick's baby brother," Aaron says. "But I want to be known as my own name."

Funny Faces — Cute Questions

Here's Aaron letting it all hang out . . . no razzle-dazzle . . . just Aaron having fun answering some silly queries!

Q: If you were an alien, what would you look like?
Aaron: "I'd have three faces. One would pop open, then another face would come out, and then a little face would come out of my mouth. The little face would have two big bulging eyes, and its eyelashes would point out really sharp — sharper than anything in the world! And his teeth would be about three inches long. I'd be a horrible alien, scaring everyone with my teeth."

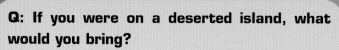

Q: If you were on a deserted island, what would you bring?
Aaron: "I would bring a big, big airplane, a lot of gas, and a speedboat that hooks onto the airplane." (And his mom's book, too.)

Q: Nick is a hottie — does it run in the family?
Aaron: (Blushing) "I guess you could say that . . . ! "

Q: Are you good friends with the Backstreet Boys?
Aaron: "Yes! I've made a nickname for them: B-HANK. B is for Brian, H is for Howie, A is for A.J., N is for Nick, and K is for Kevin."

That's all folks!

Aaron's Bulletin Board

BONUS!

Discography

Albums

Aaron Carter (1998 — Europe and USA)

Surfin' U.S.A. (1999 — Europe and USA)

Pokémon Soundtrack — (1999)

Aaron's Party (Come Get It)
(2000 — USA, Europe, Asia)

Rugrats in Paris Soundtrack (2000)

U.S. Singles

"Crush on You"

"Crazy Little Party Girl"

"That's How I Beat Shaq"

"I Want Candy"

"I'm Gonna Miss You Forever"

"Bounce"

Album Tracks

Aaron Carter

1) "I Will Be Yours"
2) "Crazy Little Party Girl"
3) "One Bad Apple"
4) "I'm Gonna Miss You Forever"
5) "Tell Me How to Make You Smile"
6) "Shake It"
7) "Please Don't Go Girl"
8) "Get Wild"
9) "I'll Do Anything"
10) "Ain't That Cute"
11) "Crush on You"
12) "Swing It Out"

Surfin' U.S.A.

1) "Surfin' U.S.A."
2) "Shake It" (Nick Carter remix)
3) "Crush on You" (Gary's mix)
4) "Crazy Little Party Girl" (One Day mix)
5) "I'm Gonna Miss You Forever" (Dream mix)
6) "Let the Music Heal Your Soul"

Aaron's Party (Come Get It)

1) "Introduction: Come to the Party"
   Interlude: Candy Call
2) "Aaron's Party (Come Get It)"
   Interlude: Candy Call
3) "I Want Candy"
   Interlude: Big Brother
4) "Bounce"
   Interlude: Yes!
5) "My Internet Girl"
   Interlude: I Can See Her Voice
6) "That's How I Beat Shaq"
   Interlude: Let's Go
7) "The Clapping Song"
   Interlude: Snappy Burger
8) "Iko Iko"
   Interlude: Teacher
9) "Real Good Time"
   Interlude: Lunch at the Studio
10) "Tell Me What You Want"
    Interlude: Stuffed!
11) "Girl You Shine"
12) "Interlude: Big Bad 'Shiney' Beat Box"

What the Future Holds for Aaron

If his multi-platinum album, *Aaron's Party (Come Get It)*, and all the things that go along with it — concert tour, personal appearances, magazine covers, etc. — aren't enough, Aaron hasn't stopped dreamin'! He's got big plans for the days to come. Here are just a few of the things Aaron has penciled in:

• *A New Album and Tour*— After Aaron's stint as Jo Jo in the Broadway musical *Suessical*, he had big plans for his next disk to get up and running. Back in April of this year he said his latest CD would be out in the fall with a tour to follow.

• *More TV Appearances* — Aaron loved doing *Sabrina the Teenage Witch* and *Lizzie McGuire,* so he is seriously considering his own sitcom . . . possibly for the 2002 TV season. "I do want to get into acting in the future," Aaron told a magazine writer recently.

• *The Big Screen* — Aaron is working on a film about a boy who meets a man suffering from cancer and comes to his aid. It was originally called *Double Take,* but another film was released under that title, so as of this writing Aaron's film is still untitled.

• *College* — Aaron wants to go to college. What would he major in? "Probably in marine biology," he says. "I've always been fascinated with underwater stuff and what's out there. There's so much we can learn that we still don't know about yet. I go scuba diving all the time, every chance I get."